SCOTTISH TARTANS

ABOVE: *Jeremiah Davison's picture shows the two MacDonald boys wearing three different tartans, none known today. From such evidence it has been* *inferred that, prior to the clans' defeat at Culloden, there was no rigid observation of clan or family tartans. This portrait, painted shortly after the Dress* *Proscription Act of 1747, could be kept with impunity since the boys' father had taken the Hanoverian side during the '45 and the family lived on Skye.*

SCOTTISH TARTANS *Alan Bold*

For such a colourful subject Scottish tartan has a mysterious past while controversy about its origins and use continues unabated to the present day. Only the future seems unquestionably bright as tartan is firmly established as an internationally successful Scottish industry and Highland dress is being increasingly adopted as a style that combines both elegance and extravagance. George Bernard Shaw, omniscient as ever, recognised this a long time ago when he said: 'The full dress of a dean is more becoming now than any other in vogue, except its one rival, the evening dress of a Scottish chieftain.'

The word 'tartan' does not exist in Gaelic and is derived from the words *tiretaine* and *tiritana* which the French and Spanish respectively used to describe a coloured woollen material. In Gaelic the word is *breacan* and was originally applied to an expansive chequered blanket. As tartan was banned for 35 years after Culloden it is often held that there is only the most tenuous or spurious connection between modern catalogues of clan tartans and the actual dress of the clansmen when the clans were a going social concern. Even if this were to be irrefutably proven it would not alter the ingenuity of the 19th-century designers so that, whether considered as an ancient or relatively modern phenomenon, the tartan is something that Scots excel at.

In a reference to the Celts in Book 8 of the *Aeneid* Virgil observes: '*Virgatis lucent sagalis*' ('Their cloaks are striped and shining'). Other references to British Celts in speckled and chequered and mottled dress suggest that tartan is an indigenously Celtic phenomenon which was so skilfully developed by the Celts of Scotland that it became the national dress of their country.

It was, however, a slow development and until the 16th century the Scottish Gael dressed in much the same fashion as his Irish counterpart. Nicolay d'Arfeville, Cosmographer to the king of France, wrote of the Scottish Highlanders in 1583: 'They wear, like the Irish, a large and full shirt, coloured with saffron, and over this a garment hanging to the knee, of thick wool, after the manner of a cassock.' Despite this Highland attachment to the saffron shirt, royalty was already using tartan as a decorative addition to courtly clothes for in 1471 James III's treasurer ordered 'Ane halve of blue Tartane to lyne his gowne of cloth of gold . . . Halve ane elne of doble Tartane to lyne ridin collars to her lade the Quene.'

By the end of the 16th century the saffron shirt was being replaced, all over the Highlands, by the *breacan feile* or belted plaid. This consisted of six ells (about five yards) of double tartan pleated and fastened round the waist by a belt so that the lower half formed a kilt and the upper half, pinned at the left shoulder with a brooch, hung down as a plaid. It not only left the arms free for work or war but could be reassembled into a blanket if the Highlander had to spend a night out in the open, a circumstance which was by no means unusual.

From the pictorial evidence of surviving portraits it is clear that the belted plaid was the everyday all-weather dress of the ordinary clansmen whereas the Highland nobility only occasionally used it—mainly for hunting. The chiefs and chieftains and gentry preferred the trews (*triubhas*). Unlike the modern regimental trews, which are really tartan trousers, the authentic trews were skintight breeches. They were more appropriate for the horseriding nobility and, because of the considerable skill needed to match the tartan sett in trews, were prized as special garments.

*

LEFT: '*A Scotch Man*' and '*A Highland Man*'. This detail from the left-hand border of a map of Scotland by John Speed (1552–1629) is one of the first depictions of tartan dress and shows an early stage in the evolution of the belted plaid.

RIGHT: Portrait of a 17th-century Highland chieftain by J. Michael Wright. This, one of the earliest pictorial records of Highland dress, shows the belted plaid worn with Restoration doublet. The chieftain—who has been inconclusively identified as Sir John Campbell of Glenorchy, 1st Earl of Breadalbane—carries the traditional arms of the Highlander: pistol, dirk, broadsword and long Spanish musket.

Atchivement of Skene of that ilk

The Highlanders were well aware that the belted plaid was considered offensive by the Lowland gentry. In 1543 John Elder, a priest, wrote to Henry VIII that 'we of all people can tolerate, suffer and always best with cold . . . going always bare legged and bare foot . . . the tender, delicate gentlemen of Scotland call us Redshanks . . . yet nevertheless . . . when we come to the Court . . . we have as good garments as some of our fellows'. And in 1578 John Lesley, bishop of Ross, confirmed this when he wrote of the Highlanders: 'If their Princes, or of their nobility, visit the King's Court, they array themselves of a courtly manner, elegantly; when they return to their country, casting off courtly decore, in all haste, they clothe themselves of their country manner.'

Exactly what stage or significance tartan itself had attained at that time is not known. The first tartans were simple checks coloured by the vegetable dyes most easily found in the district. They were made by locals for locals and became district tartans

as a rough guide to a Highlander's geographical base. However, a love of colour allied to a practical desire for camouflage made the Highlanders more adventurous and the historian George Buchanan wrote in 1581 that they 'delight in variegated garments, especially stripes, and their favourite colours are purple and red . . . but the majority now in their dress prefer a dark brown, imitating nearly the leaves of the heather, that when lying upon the heath in the day, they may not be discovered by the appearance of their clothes'.

Whether the kilt, as it is now known, had made its own appearance among these clothes is another matter. Scots are notoriously sensitive about their national identity (which many feel was taken away from them in the parliamentary Union of 1707) and it can be imagined how irritating and provocative it is for them to be told that an Englishman invented the kilt around 1727. Yet this supposed sartorial innovation has been insisted on so much that it has acquired factual status in some quarters and some

5

Scotsmen have swallowed the English kilt rather than risk eating their hats.

The *feile beag* or little kilt is derived from the kilt part of the *breacan feile* or belted plaid. It consisted of six ells of single tartan whose sewn pleats were fastened round the waist with a strap. Today the little kilt is the symbol of Scotland everywhere and it would be paradoxical indeed if it had been invented by an Englishman. Yet this was the suggestion made in the *Edinburgh Magazine* of 1785 by Ivan Baillie of Aberiachan. He claimed that around 1727 Thomas Rawlinson, manager of a Glengarry ironworks, felt his workers were too restricted in the belted plaid. He therefore dispensed with the plaid, had pleats sewn in the kilt part, and thus invented the little kilt.

By 1795 Sir John Sinclair felt qualified to say that 'it is well known that the phillibeg was invented by an Englishman in Lochaber about 60 years ago, he naturally thought his workmen could be more active in that light petticoat than in the belted plaid, and that it was more decent to wear it than to have no clothing at all, which was the case with some of those employed by him in cutting down the woods in Lochaber'. In 1845 John Sobieski Stuart's *The Costume of the Clans* repeated, as fact, the assertions about the English origins of the little kilt. The myth had snowballed its way into the national consciousness and was firmly wedged there in cold storage.

There are several reasons for doubting the integrity and motivation of the men involved in perpetrating the story. Ivan Baillie was a Hanoverian toady; Sir John Sinclair's family involvement in clearing men to make way for sheep would incline him to favour something that discredited the clansmen; John Sobieski Stuart was notoriously unreliable and always ready to put fanciful reconstruction before fact. In their attitude to the kilt these men were three of a kind and are thus unacceptable as objective witnesses.

On the other hand John Taylor's description, from his 1618 observation of the Earl of Mar's hunting party, of Highlanders wearing 'a jerkin of the same stuffe that their hose is of' suggests the little kilt, as does Thomas Kirk's phrase, in his *Account of Scotland* (1678), about 'a plad tyed about their wastes'. Though these could be confused accounts of the belted plaid it is at least arguable that they refer to the kilt and plaid as separate objects. More conclusively there was the matriculation in 1672 of the Arms of Skene of Skene. The official matriculation describes the arms being supported 'on the dexter by a Highland man in his proper garb . . . on the sinister by another in a servill habit'. The engraving of the arms made by Robert Wood between 1695 and 1704 for Nisbet's *Heraldic Plates* shows the sinister supporter wearing the little kilt.

It seems likely that the little kilt, 'a servill habit', would have economic attractions for the poorest clansmen who would find the expansive belted plaid too expensive. It is also likely that, as clansmen threw off their belted plaids before battle, the little kilt evolved as a separate item to prevent their indecent exposure. It also seems most unlikely that a sartorial invention of 1727 could have spread so rapidly by 1747 that an Act of Parliament would specifically ban the 'Philabeg, or little Kilt'. It is, therefore, sensible and safe to conclude that the belted plaid was a 16th-century improvement on the saffron shirt. That the Highland nobility were

★

the only clansmen who could afford trews for riding and for appearances at the Lowland court. That in the 17th century the little kilt developed as a separate item to be worn with or without a detachable plaid. And that both the belted plaid and the little kilt were in general use up to the battle of Culloden.

The question of clan tartans is as vexatious a subject as the development of the little kilt. From the extant pictorial evidence it seems clear that, in the pre-Culloden era, there were no rigidly observed rules for the wearing of tartans. The portrait of the MacDonald Boys shows several different tartans, all unknown today. They do, however, all have a red ground which may have been a distinctive MacDonald colour, just as Campbell tartans usually take a green ground. Then there are the ten family portraits from Grant Castle, Morayshire: all the tartans differ and none corresponds to the modern Grant tartans.

On the other hand feu duty payable to Hector MacLean in 1587 for lands in Islay took the form of sixty ells of cloth in white, black and green which corresponds to the modern Hunting MacLean tartan. So clearly some clans favoured uniformity of colour though it is extremely unlikely that any clans insisted on uniformity of sett.

One of the biggest boosts to the wearing of tartan was the parliamentary Union of 1707 which, in effect, reduced Scotland to the level of a province. Suddenly the tartan became a national symbol of patriotic disapproval of the Union. To Highlanders, who were excluded from the commercial prosperity associated with the Union, the loss of national independence simply confirmed their suspicions of the perfidious *Sassenach* —by which term they meant Lowland Scots as well as the English. And Lowlanders who disapproved of the Union took to wearing such as the Jacobite and Caledonia tartans as badges of their political allegiance.

Tartan was becoming the sartorial symbol of Scotland. In 1713 the Royal Company of Archers, a Lowland regiment, became the first governmental military body to adopt tartan as part of their uniform. And even after the 1715 Uprising the significance of tartan for Scots was accepted when the Black Watch, raised in 1729, became the first Highland regiment to wear tartan.

Disaster for the clans and their distinctive Highland dress came in 1745 in the irresistibly attractive shape of Bonnie Prince Charlie. The persecution that followed the defeat of the clans at Culloden (1746) was not merely a personal campaign by the odious 'Butcher' Cumberland, but part of government policy. They not only disarmed the clans but denied them their characteristic dress as if they wanted to wipe every feature of Gaelic culture from the face of Scotland.

Thus in 1747 the Act for the 'Abolition and Proscription of the

Highland Dress' stated that 'no man or boy within that part of Great Britain called Scotland, other than such as shall be employed as Officers and Soldiers in His Majesty's Forces, shall, on any pretext whatsoever, wear or put on the clothes commonly called Highland clothes (that is to say) the Plaid, Philabeg, or little Kilt, Trowse, Shoulder-belts, or any part whatso-ever of what peculiarly belongs to the Highland garb; and that no tartan or party-coloured plaid or stuff shall be used for Great Coats or Upper Coats'.

That, it seemed, was that. Penalties for breaking the law were six months' imprisonment for a first offence and a maximum of seven years' transportation for a second offence. However when the Act was first passed the troops were ordered to 'kill upon the spot any person whom they met dressed in the Highland garb' and this was applied even in the remote areas of the Highlands where the people had neither access to information about Acts of Parliament nor the financial

★

FACING PAGE, ABOVE LEFT: *Colonel Alasdair MacDonell of Glengarry (1771–1828), chief of the MacDonells of Glengarry, is often supposed to be the original of Fergus in Scott's* Waverley. *The high-necked tunic, the ivory-handled dirk and the sporran in this portrait by Raeburn all indicate that the costume is formal rather than functional. MacDonell appeared armed in George IV's presence during the royal visit of 1822 and, when rebuked, said, "Mac-Donell goes nowhere without his arms and his tail'.*

FACING PAGE, ABOVE RIGHT: *The Mac-nab. In the '45 rebellions the Macnab chief supported the government while his clan fought for Bonnie Prince Charlie; Raeburn's portrait shows Francis, 12th and last chief in the direct male line, who died in 1860. The pugnacious expression of the Macnab suggests his tenacious belief in a way of life that had died, with the clansmen, on the battlefield of Culloden.*

RIGHT: *George IV in Highland dress on his visit to Scotland in 1822, by Sir David Wilkie. The visit to Scotland of the first reigning monarch since Charles II, masterminded by Sir Walter Scott, did much to begin a national craze for Highland dress and tartan. The king appeared in Highland dress and expected his Scottish subjects to follow suit. On the occasion of this visit Scott proclaimed the king as 'our kinsman . . . we are the* clan *and our King is the Chief'.*

9

wherewithal to acquire instantly a new outfit.

It will be noticed that women were excluded from the terms of the Act. Wealthy Highland women had long worn elaborate dresses and *arisaid* plaids; clanswomen went bareheaded (and barefoot) before marriage but had a post-marital linen *curac* to cover the head. This style was not, however, encouraged in the Lowlands. In 1631 Edinburgh women were forbidden to wear plaids over their heads and in 1648 the same city ordered prompt punishment—£5 fine and confiscation of the offending garment—for women persisting with their illegal head-covering. And, of course, the Dress Proscription Act did not help. Ramsey of Ochtertyre, writing in 1785, said that 'in 1747, when I first knew Edinburgh, nine-tenths of the ladies still wore plaids, especially at church . . . so rapidly did the plaid wear out, that when I returned to Edinburgh in 1752 one could hardly see a lady in that piece of dress'.

In fact active persecution of High-

★

ABOVE: *Pipers at Pitlochry. Something of the old stirring clan spirit is simulated in modern Highland gatherings like this one at Pitlochry in 1964. It was near Pitlochry, at Killiecrankie on 27 July 1689, that Viscount Dundee—who had taken up arms in the cause of the exiled King James II—defeated government troops under General MacKay, a victory nullified by Dundee's death in battle.*

land dress virtually stopped when George III came to the throne in 1760. George was fascinated by the romance of the Stuarts and had, in his Scottish Prime Minister Lord Bute, a man well aware of the unnecessary hostility created by the existence of the Dress Proscription Act. In the more relaxed atmosphere the Highland Society of London (founded 1778) appointed a committee to fight for the repeal of the Act. This was achieved in 1782 when the Marquis of Graham, M.P. (later Duke of Montrose), introduced a repeal Bill which passed unopposed through both Houses of Parliament.

An indication of what this must have meant to the Highlanders can be gathered from the Gaelic proclamation circulated to announce the repeal. 'Listen, Men!', it began, 'This is bringing before all the Sons of the Gael that the King and Parliament of Britain have for ever abolished the Act against the Highland Dress that came down to the Clans from the beginning of the world to the year 1746. This must bring great joy to every Highland heart. You are no longer bound down to the unmanly dress of the Lowlander.' However in the 35 years that the ban had been in force many 'Sons of the Gael' had been cleared out of their homes or had long since decided to emigrate. Highland dress did not immediately revive. It took the showmanship of a great novelist and the willing co-

operation of a king to put tartan back on the map of Scotland.

Sir Walter Scott remade Scotland in his own image in many ways. He was not only a celebrated writer but an immensely influential man. He personally persuaded George IV to visit Scotland and become the first reigning monarch to do so since the time of Charles II. Furthermore he persuaded George to appear in kilt and plaid and let the Highland gentry know that they would be expected to do likewise. George IV revelled in the occasion and this 1822 visit virtually initiated the tartan industry so great was its impact. The firm of William Wilson & Son of Bannockburn, who had an insignificant list of tartans in 1800, manufactured about 150 at the time of the royal visit. In 1842 the Sobieski Stuart brothers published their huge catalogue of tartans, *Vestiarium Scoticum,* which is more impressive for its inventiveness than for its authenticity.

The trend started by George IV was continued by Victoria and Albert. After spending a holiday at Balmoral with the Queen, Albert bought the 24,000-acre Aberdeenshire estate in 1852. He not only commissioned a new castle but designed a tartan to be the exclusive property of the Royal Family. This Balmoral sett is attractive evidence of Albert's devotion to Scotland, however romantic his conception of Scottish history might have been. It also shows that there is nothing objectionable about a modern design of tartan.

Some authorities argue that only those with a clan or sept right to a tartan are entitled to wear one. They believe in the MacDonald tartan for the MacDonalds, the MacGregor tartan for the MacGregors—and the general tartans, like the Jacobite or Caledonia, for the rest of us. This seems an unjustifiably élitist view of the subject and one that cannot be based on the documentary history of the tartans.

It is, after all, established that most of the setts now known were designed after the repeal of the Dress Proscription Act in 1782. It is also known that the clan chiefs, who were after all the genuine Gaelic article, did not scrupulously adhere to any single sett. And if they could choose according to what their eyes beheld as beautiful it would be wrong to deny this right to people today. The fact is that people can and do buy tartans that appeal to them and wear them without worrying too much if they are treading on anyone's genealogical brogues.

Those interested in a particular clan often choose to wear its tartan and this seems as good a reason for wearing the tartan as any. Certainly the huge lists of clan septs compiled by manufacturers and retailers of tartans are not always convincing and it is absurd to insist dogmatically that the wearer of a tartan must have at least a sept right when this sept may be the whim of a retailer. Furthermore, attempts to make a universally acceptable sett have been doomed to oblivion.

Today there are more than 1,000 tartans which is evidence of the enormous interest in and enduring appeal of the subject. Those who want to impose a clan monopoly on a particular tartan are surely doing down Scotland's gift to the world and those ancestors they claim to revere. As Allan Ramsay said in his poem 'Tartana':

Antiquity contains a certain spell,
To make ev'n things of little
    worth excel;
To smallest subjects gives a glaring
    dash,
Protecting high-born idiots from
    the lash.

Tartan is too attractive to be confined to Scotland. In a country not noted for visual achievements it is a reminder of a natural flair for colour. It is also a permanent reminder of a painful history. Most of all the tartan brings the colours of the Highlands into the drab city environment and from there hitches itself a lift on the waists of the world's romantics.

ACKNOWLEDGMENTS
The Balmoral tartan on p. 13 is reproduced by gracious permission of Her Majesty the Queen. The copyright illustrations of Scottish tartans are reproduced by courtesy of Kinloch Anderson Ltd, of Edinburgh. At their head office in George Street, Edinburgh, and in their American store in Alexandria, Virginia, interested enquirers may view and buy the world's finest range of authentic clan and family tartans. Other illustrations are acknowledged as follows: front cover and p. 10, British Tourist Authority; pp. 1, 3, 4 and 7, Scottish National Portrait Gallery; pp. 2, 5 (left) and back cover, National Library of Scotland; p. 5 (right), National Museum of Antiquities of Scotland; p. 6, Royal Company of Archers; p. 8 (left), National Gallery of Scotland; p. 8 (right), John Dewar and Sons Ltd, Distillers; p. 9, the Royal Collection, by gracious permission of Her Majesty the Queen; p. 11 (top), Patrick Lichfield; p. 11 (bottom), John Scott; photographs on pp. 1, 6 and 7 by Tom Scott. The publishers would also like to acknowledge the assistance provided by the Scottish Tartans Society, of Comrie, Perthshire, the only research and museum body exclusively devoted to tartans and Highland dress.

TOP: *The Royal Family's close Scottish connections and great sartorial influence have done much to promote the wearing of tartans. This picture was taken in 1972 at Balmoral.*
ABOVE: *The Balmoral tartan, which is reserved exclusively for the use of members of the Royal Family, was designed by Prince Albert and named after the 'dear paradise' he created for Queen Victoria on their Aberdeenshire estate. Prince Charles and Prince Edward are here seen wearing the tartan at the Braemar Games.*

Anderson

Whether as Lowland Anderson or Highland MacAndrew, the family of the 'son of Andrew' is as familiar throughout Scotland as the name of the patron saint from whom their own name is sometimes said to derive. The MacAndrews, a Badenoch sept of Clan Chattan, produced the great archer Iain Beg MacAindrea (Little John Anderson). In response to a cattle raid of 1670 Iain and some associates tracked the Lochaber raiders to their hideaway bothy up in Strathdearn. Only one of the raiders survived Iain's arrows—the sentry who ran away to tell the tale. Iain himself survived several attempts to avenge his deadly display of archery.

MOTTO: *Stand sure.*

Armstrong

One of the most powerful of Border clans is traditionally descended from the astonishingly muscular armour-bearer Fairbairn who, finding a Scottish king unhorsed in battle, lifted him effortlessly on to his own horse. The reward was the eponym and lands in the Borders where an Armstrong of Liddesdale is recorded in 1376. The turbulent behaviour of the clan led to James V ordering the summary execution of John Armstrong of Gilnockie and his men at Carlingrigg in 1530, an event lamented in the ballad 'Johnie Armstrong'. The name was immortalised by the first man on the moon, Neil Armstrong.

MOTTO: *Invictus maneo (I remain unvanquished).*

Balmoral

Unless you happen to be a member of the Royal Family this is one tartan you certainly may *not* wear. Prince Albert bought the 24,000-acre Aberdeenshire estate of Balmoral in 1852, commissioned a grandiose new castle, and personally supervised every detail of Victoria's 'dear paradise'. He also personally designed this tartan. Balmoral remains the favourite Scottish retreat of the Royal Family and the Balmoral tartan is reserved exclusively for their use. Although some Scots were outraged at the title Elizabeth II when there had never been a royal Scottish Elizabeth, the Royal Family's Scottish connections and sartorial influence have helped to promote the wearing of tartans.

Black Watch

The 42nd Royal Highland Regiment was the first Highland regiment to wear tartan yet, despite the strong regimental associations, the Black Watch tartan is a suitable choice for those with no clan or sept claim to a tartan. The regiment was raised by General Wade in 1729 to prevent clans levying protection-money on cattle, and there was a noticeable decrease in cattle raiding until the Black Watch left Scotland to fight in Europe as part of the British Army. Their tartan so differed from the red coat of the British regulars that the regiment became known as the *Freicea-dan Dubh* (Black Watch).

MOTTO: *Nemo me impune lacessit (No one attacks me with impunity).*

Bruce

Sir Robert de Brus, a Norman knight, came to England with William the Conqueror and his son Robert went to Scotland with David I who granted him the Lordship of Annandale. Robert, 7th Lord of Annandale, unsuccessfully claimed the Scottish throne in 1290, took part in Wallace's campaign of 1297 and, after the execution of Wallace in 1305, personally led a national campaign for independence which culminated in his victory over Edward II at Bannockburn in 1314. The Treaty of Northampton, 1328, recognised Bruce as king of an independent Scotland. Bruce's body is buried at Dunfermline and his heart is buried at Melrose.

MOTTO: *Fuimus (We have been).*

Buchanan

Descended from Anselan O'Kyan, son of a king of Ulster, who was granted the lands of Buchanan on the eastern shores of Loch Lomond by Malcolm II, the clan was renowned for its skill in battle. From their meeting place on the tiny Loch Lomond island of Clairinch they would set out. They supported Bruce and their clan chief fell at Flodden. The name is a famous one. George Buchanan, poet and scholar, was tutor to Mary Queen of Scots and James VI. James Buchanan was 15th President of the U.S.A. World lightweight champion Ken Buchanan fought in Buchanan tartan boxing trunks.

MOTTO: *Clarior hinc honos (Brighter hence the honour).*

Caledonia

Like Jacobite this is a general tartan with no clan significance and so may be legitimately worn by those with no clan or sept claim to a tartan. It has been linked with those Scottish emigrants who, in 1698, disastrously failed in their attempt to establish the colony of Caledonia in Darien. Unlike the Jacobite tartan, the Caledonia has no connection with the Stuart cause though it was probably likewise worn by Lowlanders in the 18th century to signify disapproval of the parliamentary Union of 1707. According to the authoritative Lord Lyon, surname alone determines the right to a tartan so Scots with no clan surnames, no Jacobite sentiments and no district affiliations should wear the Caledonia.

Cameron

The name of this clan, renowned for its extraordinarily ferocious fighting ability, means 'crooked nose' (*Camsron*)—a description of a 14th-century chief. In 1370 at Inverhavon, in a dispute over lands in Lochaber, they took on the Clan Chattan confederation and crushed the Davidsons and Mackintoshes before the Macphersons intervened. After a meeting with Bonnie Prince Charlie in 1745 Donald Cameron of Lochiel, most respected of Highland chiefs, impulsively committed the clan to the Jacobite cause and thus made the '45 possible. Their war cry was '*Chlanna nan con thigibh a so's gheibh sibh feoil!*' ('Sons of the hound come and get flesh!')

MOTTO: *Aonaibh ri cheile (Unite).*

Cameron of Erracht

This is a military, not a clan, tartan. The Queen's Own Cameron Highlanders (originally the 79th Highlanders) were raised by Sir Alan Cameron of Erracht in 1793. Sir Alan, who had served in America, was a vigorous campaigner against the laws proscribing Highland dress. It is regimental tradition that Sir Alan's mother, Marsali, conceived this popular MacDonald-inspired tartan. The Camerons of Erracht date from the 16th century and their chief was second-in-command when the Camerons were out in the '45. Erracht was adopted as a day tartan by many Camerons before Lochiel approved the Hunting Cameron in 1956.

REGIMENTAL MOTTO: *Cameron.*

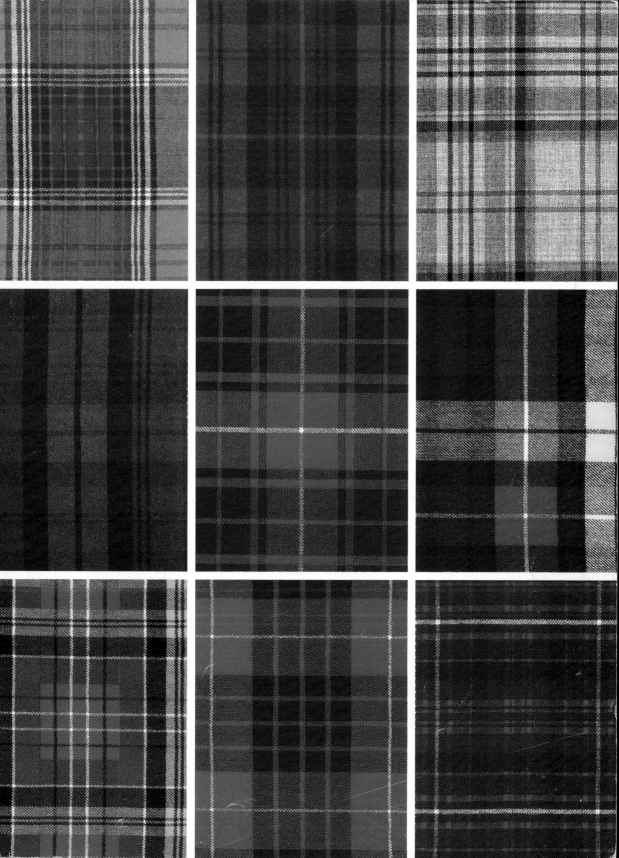

Campbell of Argyll

From Sir Colin Campbell of Lochawe (13th century) came this clan whose chiefs were henceforth designated *Mac Chailein Mor* (Son of Big Colin). During the Civil War they identified with the Protestant cause and supported Cromwell against Charles I. William of Orange created the 1st Duke of Argyll and the clan became the most powerful anti-Jacobite force in Scotland. John, 2nd Duke, a formidable soldier, did much to extinguish Jacobite hopes in 1715; and John, 4th Duke, raised the Scottish militia during the '45 and took over from Cumberland in pacifying the Highlands. Gaelic *Cambeul* means 'crooked mouth'.

MOTTO: *Ne obliviscaris (Forget not).*

Campbell of Breadalbane

The head of the Glenorchy branch of Clan Campbell is *Mac Chailein Mhic Dhonnachaidh* (son of Colin Duncan's son) after Sir Colin, son of Sir Duncan Campbell of Lochawe, who inherited Glenorchy and added land in Lorn through marriage, whence the clan expanded at the expense of their neighbours: they had the 10th MacGregor chief executed before an invited audience in 1570. Sir John Campbell, 1st Earl of Breadalbane (1681), was 'cunning as a fox, wise as a serpent, and slippery as an eel'. He refused to account for the government money given him to buy loyalty from the clans and certainly approved the massacre of Glencoe.

MOTTO: *Follow me.*

Chisholm

Of Norman origin, the Chisholms were associated with Berwickshire and with Roxburghshire where the feudal barony of Chiesholme was situated. When Sir Robert de Chisholme became Constable of Urquhart Castle, on Loch Ness, in 1359 the family used their Highland base to establish themselves in Erchless and Strathglass in Inverness-shire. In 1715 some 200 clansmen fought at Sheriffmuir and, in 1746, the clan performed with considerable courage in the circumstances of Culloden. One of the Seven Men of Glenmoriston, the guerilla band who led Bonnie Prince Charlie to Arisaig, was a Chisholm.

MOTTO: *Feros ferio (I am fierce with the fierce).*

Clan Chattan

This was not a clan but a confederation of clans under Mackintosh hegemony comprising the Mackintoshes, Davidsons, Macphersons, MacGillivrays and MacBeans—though membership was later extended to such as the Farquharsons. In 1291 Angus, 6th Mackintosh chief, married the Clan Chattan heiress Eva—daughter of Dougall Dall—and became Captain of Clan Chattan. In 1938 the 28th Mackintosh chief died without naming his Clan Chattan successor and in 1947 the Lyon Court granted the chiefship to a descendant of the Daviot branch of the Mackintoshes.

MOTTO: *Touch not the cat but [without] a glove.*

Colquhoun

Named after the Dunbartonshire lands of Colquhoun, the clan acquired Luss through marriage and, in 1602, determined to protect their Loch Lomondside interests by attacking their MacGregor neighbours. In the resulting battle at Glenfruin 200 Colquhouns were slaughtered for the loss of two MacGregors, a massacre that moved the king to outlaw the MacGregors. Never again were the Colquhouns taken seriously as a fighting force, though they made some impact in politics. Sir John, 19th of Luss, baronet of Nova Scotia, had to flee the country after sexual indiscretions but Sir John, 20th of Luss, was a member of parliament.

MOTTO: *Si je puis (If I can).*

Crawford

The family are so called after the feudal barony of Crawford in the Upper Ward of Clydesdale and there is documentary evidence for the existence of one Galfridus de Crawford around 1179. In 1248 Sir John Crawford of that Ilk left two daughters and the Earls of Crawford are descended from the marriage of the youngest daughter to David Lindsay of Wauchopedale. Sir Archibald Crawford of Loudon, Sheriff of Ayr, was murdered by the English at a banquet in Ayr in 1297. His sister, Margaret, married a Wallace and became mother of the national hero William Wallace.

MOTTO: *Tutum te robore reddam (I will make thee safe by my strength).*

Culloden

This sett is based on a tartan fragment discovered, in 1946, deep in the peat of Culloden Moor, and 'Reproduction' tartans generally derive from its subdued colours. The battle of Culloden of 1746, which lasted only 25 minutes, was a total disaster for Gaelic Scotland. Cumberland's victory over the Jacobites was followed by a period of persecution so intense that the clan system, which had long irritated Hanoverian governments, was finally destroyed. It was after Culloden, too, that Parliament proscribed Highland dress—a ban not lifted until 1782. Thus there is much controversy, and little documentary evidence, about the clan significance of tartans before the '45.

Cunningham

Cunningham is a district in Ayrshire and Hervey de Cunningham was given Kilmaurs by Alexander III for bravery at Largs in 1263. Marriage to an heiress added to the estates and the 1st Earl of Glencairn was created in 1488. The family have long been friends of the famous. The 4th Earl was close to John Knox and the 9th Earl, William Cunningham, was appointed Lord Chancellor after the Restoration. James, 14th Earl Glencairn, was an enthusiastic patron of Burns, welcoming him into Edinburgh society and raising subscriptions for a new edition of the poems. Burns wrote a 'Lament' on his death, since when the earldom has been dormant.

MOTTO: *Over fork over.*

Davidson

Named after their first chief, David Dubh of Invernahaven, the clan entered the Clan Chattan confederation in the 14th century when a Davidson chief married the daughter of a Mackintosh chief. Responding to a Cameron attack of 1370 the Mackintosh rallied Clan Chattan and the Davidsons were given place of honour on his right, a slight that made the Macphersons withdraw. Clan Chattan were defeated and the Davidsons decimated. To settle their quarrel selected Davidsons and Macphersons met on Perth's North Inch in 1396 in a fight to the death in which the Davidsons were defeated.

MOTTO: *Sapienter si sincere (Wisely if sincerely).*

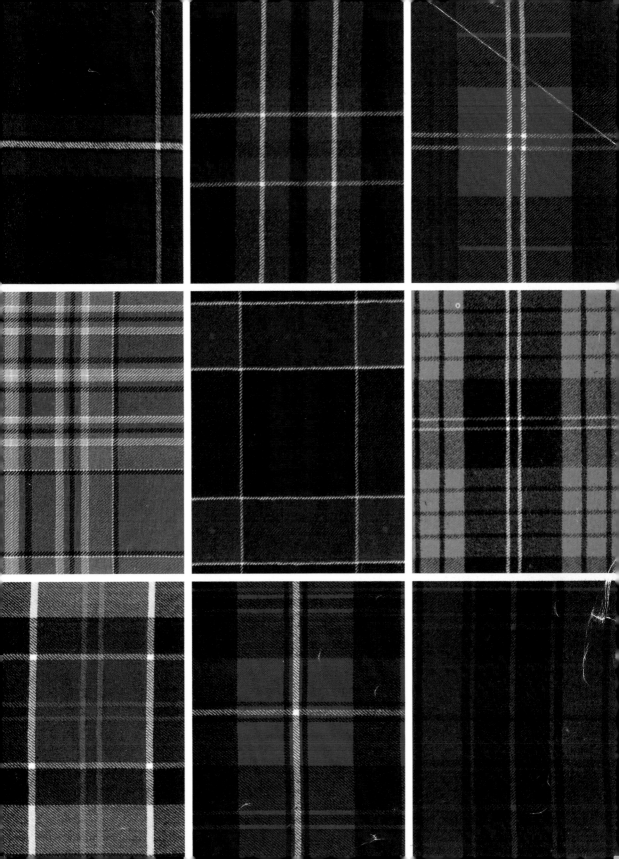

Drummond

The Drummonds have their territorial origins in the Stirlingshire lands of Drymen which were held by their 13th-century ancestor Maelcolum Beg ('Little Malcolm'). After Bannockburn, where he supported Bruce, Sir Malcolm of Drummond was rewarded with land in Perthshire. The Drummond ladies were conspicuously beautiful: Margaret Drummond married David II; Annabella Drummond married Robert III and was mother of James I. The Drummonds were loyal to Mary Queen of Scots and the exiled James II for which they were created Jacobite dukes. In the '15 and the '45 the 2nd and 3rd Dukes fought on the Jacobite side.

MOTTO: *Gang warily (Go carefully).*

Farquharson

An Aberdeenshire clan of the Clan Chattan confederation, they take their name from a 15th-century forester, Farquhar. Through marriage Donald, 4th chief, gained Invercauld as clan seat. Finlay Mor, 5th chief, died carrying the royal standard at Pinkie (1547). Loyal to the Stuarts, the clan fought under Montrose and Dundee and, in 1715, at Preston. When, in the '45, the 22nd Mackintosh chief opposed the Stuarts his wife, a Farquharson of Invercauld, led the clan. As hostess to Prince Charles, 'Colonel Anne' organised the Rout of Moy when five of her men scared off a large Hanoverian force.

MOTTO: *Fide et fortitudine (By fidelity and fortitude).*

Fergusson

The original Son of Fergus is untraced, though groups of Fergussons proliferated throughout Scotland. Fergusson of Kilkerran (Ayrshire) came to be accepted as clan chief and the Kilkerran branch produced a steady stream of distinguished public men. Scattered as they were, the clan never united in a cause and Captain John Ferguson, who in his sloop *Furnace* hunted the fugitive Prince Charlie, has come down in Scottish history as a villain. However there is Robert Fergusson, the vernacular poet who inspired Burns; Adam Ferguson, the philosopher; and 'Bonnie Annie Laurie', wife of a Fergusson.

MOTTO: *Dulcius ex asperis (Sweeter after difficulties).*

Forbes

Forbes is a parish in Aberdeenshire traditionally made fit for human habitation when Oconochar killed a local bear and went on to found this clan. Feudal tenure of the lands was confirmed in 1271. Alexander Forbes, 4th Lord Pitsligo, lost his estates for his part in the '45. Duncan Forbes of Culloden, Lord President of the Court of Session, first dissuaded many clans from joining an apparently hopeless cause in 1745, then tried, in vain, to persuade the government to firmly admonish rather than brutally punish the defeated Jacobites. George II would not listen to reason. Lord Forbes, clan chief, lives on Donside near the famous Castle of Craigievar.

MOTTO: *Grace me guide.*

Fraser

The first recorded Highland Fraser is Sir Andrew, who obtained the lands of Lovat by marriage, and the clan gained a reputation for equivocation: they opposed Montrose but supported Dundee. Simon Fraser, Lord Lovat, 14th chief, was outlawed for outrageous behaviour and, while Jacobite in the company of influential Jacobites, he so professed the opposite that William of Orange granted a pardon. 'The Old Fox' helped initiate the 1715 Uprising, then, when it was clearly doomed, helped put it down. In the '45 he declared himself a Jacobite when the Jacobites triumphed at Prestonpans and for this was, at 80, the last man beheaded in England.

MOTTO: *Je suis prest (I am ready).*

Gordon

Though Lowland in origin the family became established in Aberdeenshire when Bruce granted lands to Sir Adam of Gordon. Elizabeth, a 15th-century Gordon heiress, married Alexander Seton and their son retained the Gordon name—becoming clan chief, the Earl of Huntly. The Gordons were dominant throughout their area and the chiefs styled themselves 'Cock o' the North'. The famous Gordon Highlanders were raised by the 4th Duke in 1794 though his wife, the Duchess Jane, should get some of the credit. Apparently her recruiting technique was to pass a guinea from her lips to the lips of each new Gordon Highlander.

MOTTO: *Bydand (Remaining).*

Graham of Montrose

The first recorded Scottish Graham is William de Graham to whom David I gave Abercorn and Dalkeith. Sir John Graham of Dundaff died at Falkirk in 1298 and the 1st Earl of Montrose at Flodden in 1513, but James Graham, 1st Marquis of Montrose, was the finest soldier of them all. As Charles I's lieutenant-general in Scotland he led the Highlanders in a magnificent series of victories. John Graham of Claverhouse, 'Bonnie Dundee', who died winning the battle of Killiecrankie in 1689, carried on the family tradition. The 3rd Duke of Montrose, an M.P., helped to ensure the repeal of the act proscribing Highland dress.

MOTTO: *Ne oublie (Do not forget).*

Grant

Sir Laurence le Grant established a Highland foothold when he became sheriff of Inverness (c .1258) and a succeeding sheriff, Sir Iain Grant, obtained lands in Strathspey by marriage. By the 16th century the chiefs were Lairds of Grant. As a reward for support of William of Orange a semi-autonomous Regality of Grant was established and the Grants (the Glenmoriston Grants excepted) remained anti-Jacobite. In 1820, when Tory headquarters at Grant Lodge were blockaded by the Whigs of Elgin, for the last time in Highland history the fiery cross went out and 800 Grant clansmen lifted the blockade in response.

MOTTO: *Stand fast.*

Gunn

A Caithness and Sutherland clan descended from Olaf the Black, a 13th-century Norse king, the Gunns in the 15th century endlessly disputed land with the Keiths of Ackergill until clan chief Crowner George Gunn invited twelve Keith horsemen to meet twelve Gunn horsemen at St. Tyer Chapel near Wick in 1464. The Keiths came two to a horse and slaughtered the Gunns. In 1520 at Drummoy the Gunns in turn slaughtered fourteen Keiths. They then turned their fury on the Earls of Caithness and Sutherland but were defeated at Lochbroom in 1585 by their many enemies.

MOTTO: *Aut pax aut bellum (Either peace or war).*

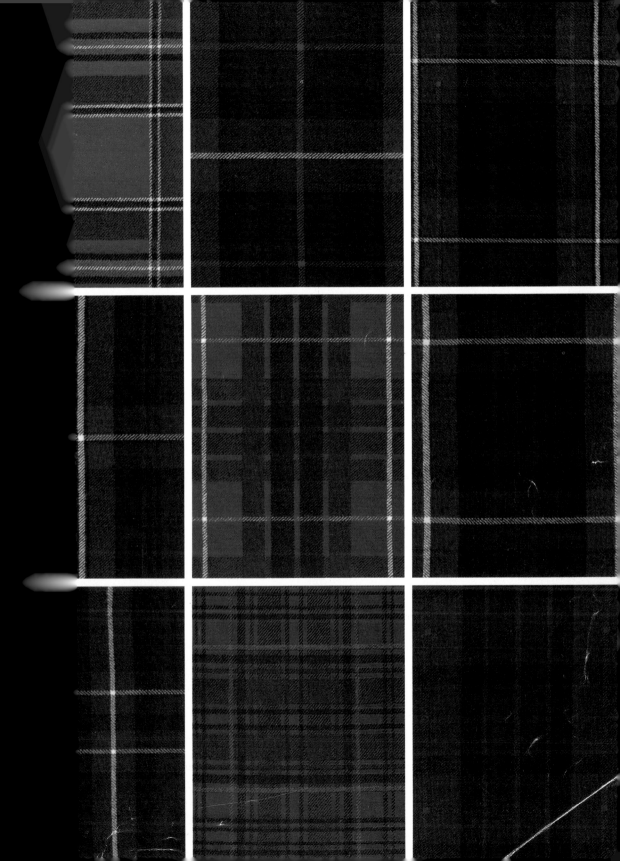

Jacobite

This is a general tartan, with no clan or district significance, and can therefore legitimately be worn by those with no clan or sept claim to a tartan. After the parliamentary Union of 1707 this tartan was worn by nationalistic Lowlanders as a gesture of protest against the loss of Scottish independence. In particular it was observed on the plaids of the ladies of Edinburgh. In the 1715 Uprising the tartan was worn by some Lowland sympathisers with the Jacobite cause, hence the name. As many new tartans were invented in the popular aftermath of George IV's visit to Scotland in 1822, one of the attractions of the Jacobite tartan is its undoubted antiquity.

Lindsay

Since the time of the seminal 11th-century Anglo-Norman baron, Baldric de Lindesay, the family established themselves from Crawford in Lanarkshire to Strathnairn in Inverness-shire and the militant Sir David Lindsay, champion tourneyer of Scotland, was created 1st Earl of Crawford in 1398. The family abounds in characters. 'Beardie', the 4th Earl, plotted with Douglas and Ross to divide up Scotland among themselves: they were defeated by Huntly at Brechin in 1452. Alexander, 'the Wicked Master', son of the 8th Earl, was an aspiring patricide, Sir David Lindsay of the Mount (1490–1555) a poet.

MOTTO: *Endure fort (Endure with strength)*.

MacDonald

Donald, grandson of King Somerled of the Isles, founded this clan and built a power base from his inheritance of Islay and Kintyre. Donald's son, Angus *mor*, the first MacDonald, reluctantly submitted to the crown in 1263 and set a precedent for the clan's persistent opposition to central authority. At Culloden in 1746 Lord George Murray caused unnecessary resentment by putting the clan on the left wing though, since Bannockburn, they had taken their place on the right. The name spans Highland history, from the tragic massacre of Glencoe (1692) to the selfless courage of Flora MacDonald.

MOTTO: *Per mare per terras (By sea and by land)*.

MacDonald of Clanranald

Ranald, younger son of the 1st Lord of the Isles, founded this branch of Clan Donald and, from the beginning, the clan fought among themselves for hierarchical rights. The sadistic 6th chief was killed by the clan and in 1544 the Battle of the Shirts (so called because the intense heat made the participants strip) was fought to determine the chiefship of the clan in favour of John of Moidart. The 13th chief was killed at Sheriffmuir fighting for the Stuarts and it was on Clanranald territory at Glenfinnan that Bonnie Prince Charlie raised his standard in 1745 and from Clanranald territory in the Hebrides that he planned his escape from Scotland.

MOTTO: *My hope is constant in thee.*

MacDonald of the Isles

When John MacDonald of Islay assumed the title *Dominus Insularum* in 1354 he directly challenged the authority of the crown. The MacDonalds were the most powerful clan, controlling most of the western seaboard—but that was not enough. Donald, 2nd Lord of the Isles, signed a treaty with the English king, claimed the vacant Earldom of Ross, and pressed his claim at the battle of Harlaw in 1411. The indecisive result meant that Donald became a vassal of the Scottish crown. In 1493 James IV abolished the Lordship of the Isles and the title is now the purely nominal possession of the Prince of Wales.

MOTTO: *Per mare per terras (By sea and by land)*.

MacDougall

Dougall, son of King Somerled of the Isles, founded the MacDougalls of Lorn. In an assassination attempt on Bruce three MacDougall clansmen were killed but one died grasping Bruce's brooch, still the clan's prized possession. The clan suffered for their opposition to Bruce until Ewan, 5th chief, married one of Bruce's granddaughters. Ewan left no heir and the Stewarts of Durrisdeer and Innermeath inherited Lorn, though in 1457 a MacDougall was granted Dunollie, henceforth the clan seat. For their part in the 1715 Rising their lands were forfeited but given back when they joined the Hanoverians in 1745.

MOTTO: *Buaidh no bàs (Victory or death)*.

MacFarlane

The name *Mac Pharlain* means 'son of Parlan (Bartholomew)' and the original Parlan was a great-grandson of 13th-century Alwyn, Earl of Lennox. The clan became a notorious fighting force around Loch Lomond and took part in the battle of Pinkie (1547) and the battle of Langside (1568) where they opposed Queen Mary and captured three of her standards. The activities of the clan were frequently outrageously illegal and the conviction of MacFarlane clansmen for armed robbery in 1624 was no isolated incident. As a bizarre tribute to the shady nocturnal adventures of the clan the local Scots nicknamed the moon 'MacFarlane's lantern'.

MOTTO: *This I'll defend.*

MacGregor

Despite their claim to royal descent from Gregor, Kenneth MacAlpin's brother, this clan are remembered for being outlawed for 139 years. Because the MacGregors held land on the clan principle alone, the Campbells were able to appropriate their possessions until the MacGregor chief became a mere tenant of Campbell of Glenorchy. After one massive cattle raid the MacGregors had to confront and slaughter the outraged Colquhouns at Glenfruin in 1603. A furious James VI had the clan outlawed and the name abolished. When reinstated in 1775, 826 clansmen acknowledged themselves.

MOTTO: *'S rioghal mo dhream (Royal is my race)*.

MacKay

The name *Mac Aoidh* means 'son of Hugh', a reference to the grandson of 14th-century Morgan (the clan have also been known as Clan Morgan). They unsuccessfully attempted to halt the Lord of the Isles's advance in 1411 and did badly in their long armed struggle to protect Strathnaver, the MacKay country, from the Earls of Sutherland. Abroad Sir Donald MacKay in 1626 raised 3,000 men for service in Bohemia; and Aeneas, of the MacKay Dutch Regiment, was created a Dutch baron. In 1642 Strathnaver had to be sold and in 1829 the Sutherland family acquired the remaining MacKay lands.

MOTTO: *Manu forti (With a strong hand)*.

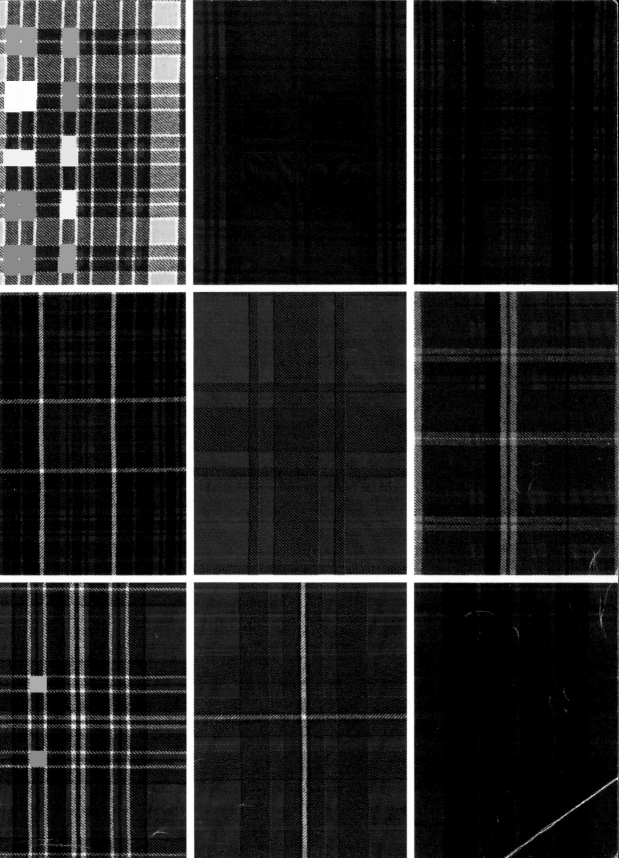

MacKenzie

The territorially ambitious Mac-Kenzies expanded from their original home in Kintail in Wester Ross until they stretched from the east coast to Lewis. Kenneth MacKenzie was created Lord of Kintail in 1609 and his son, Colin, became Earl of Seaforth in 1623. The 3rd Earl of Seaforth's wife had a clansman, Kenneth the Brahan Seer, burned for witchcraft; most details of his macabre last prophecy were fulfilled, including the untimely deaths of all four of the last Earl of Seaforth's sons before his own in 1815. The National Trust for Scotland now own Kintail estate (14,000 acres).

MOTTO: *Luceo non uro (I shine, not burn)*.

Mackintosh

The name *Mac-an-Toisich* ('son of the Thane') described 13th-century Shaw MacDuff, son of the Earl of Fife, and the clan assumed leadership of Clan Chattan when Angus, 6th chief, married Eva, the confederation's heiress, in 1291. Subsequently the Mackintosh was also Captain of Clan Chattan and, as such, participated in territorial feuds: the last clan battle, at Mulroy in 1688, was between the Mackintoshes and (victorious) Mac-Donalds of Keppoch over land in Lochaber. The Mackintosh supported William III but in 1715 the clan, under Brigadier Mackintosh of Borlum, followed the Old Pretender.

MOTTO: *Touch not the cat bot [without] a glove.*

MacLean

Founded by 13th-century Gilleathain na Tuaidh (Gillian of the Battleaxe) the clan became established in the Western Isles as supporters of the MacDonald Lords of the Isles. As such they fought, and lost their chief, at the battle of Red Harlaw in 1411. Their war-cry was used in battle against Cromwell's General Lambert at Inverkeithing in 1651, when Hector, 18th chief, was protected by seven brothers. As each one fell another took his place shouting *'Fear eile airson Eachainn!'* ('Another for Hector') though Hector, alas, also died. In 1910 the 13th-century Duart Castle on Mull, home of the clan chiefs, was reacquired by the MacLeans.

MOTTO: *Virtue mine honour.*

Hunting MacLeod (Harris)

Tormod and Torquil, the sons of Leod (13th-century son of a Norse king), founded the two main branches of the MacLeods: Harris and Lewis. The MacLeods of Harris, styling themselves the MacLeods of Mac-Leod, were Clan Tormod and fought with Bruce at Bannockburn. Their ancestral home, Dunvegan Castle in Skye, is the most famous clan seat and has been continuously occupied by the family for the last seven centuries. Near Dunvegan Alasdair, the 8th chief (1481–1547), established a college of piping. After losing hundreds of clansmen supporting the Stuarts at Worcester in 1651, the clan remained neutral during the '45.

MOTTO: *Hold fast.*

Dress MacLeod (Lewis)

Clan Torquil, the MacLeods of Lewis, were supporters of the Mac-Donald Lords of the Isles and, even after the forfeiture of 1493, plotted to restore the Lordship. The history of the Lewis MacLeods is, in fact, one of internal dispute and external feud culminating in a confrontation with the crown and the territorially ambitious MacKenzies. As a result the Lewis chief himself was forfeited and many of his family killed. Thereafter the MacLeods of Raasay assumed leadership of the branch and 100 of them supported the Jacobite cause in 1745. A century later, in 1846, the 11th Laird was obliged to sell the island of Raasay.

MOTTO: *Hold fast.*

Macmillan

It is probable that this clan descends from a Celtic monastic family as *Mac Mhaolain* means 'son of the tonsured one'. The family came to be associated with Knapdale where there is a Macmillan's Tower in Castle Sween and Macmillan's Cross in Kilmory Knap churchyard. Traditionally there was also a sea-rock whose carved Gaelic inscription proclaimed the family rights as long as the waves kept beating. As well as giving their name to an American town and a Canadian river, the family produced the inventor of the pedal bicycle Kirkpatrick Macmillan and the British Prime Minister Harold Macmillan.

MOTTO: *Miseris succerrere disco (I learn to succour the distressed).*

Macnab

This nominally ecclesiastical clan— *Mac an Aba* means 'son of the Abbot' —descended from the abbots of Glendochart, showed far from divine judgment when they supported the MacDougalls against the Bruce, losing everything but the barony of Bovain, Glendochart. A pro-Stuart Macnab chief, 'Smooth John', was killed at Worcester in 1651 and the chiefs held back in 1715 and 1745 although their clansmen fought for the Jacobite cause. The sternly eccentric features of Francis, 16th chief, are preserved in Raeburn's full-length portrait 'The Macnab'. Although he never married, he produced 32 children.

MOTTO: *Timor omnis abesto (Let fear be far from all).*

Macpherson

The original 'son of the parson' was Donald, son of Duncan, a 15th-century parson of Kingussie. As one of the original branches of Clan Chattan the Macphersons constantly challenged the Mackintosh leadership. Within the family the Macphersons of Cluny dominated. Most famous was Ewen Macpherson of Cluny who led about 400 of the clan behind Bonnie Prince Charlie in the '45. After Culloden he went underground for nine years, living in Cluny's Cage, a cave on the slopes of Ben Alder, which is described as 'a nest upon a cliff-side' in Stevenson's *Kidnapped*. Eventually he escaped to France, where he died.

MOTTO: *Touch not the cat bot [without] a glove.*

Dress Macpherson

Ewen, grandson of Cluny Macpherson of the '45, was recognised by the Lord Lyon as chief of clan Macpherson in 1873 and thereafter lived what he took to be the life of a Highland chief. Fascinated by Macpherson history he was convinced of the authenticity of the Macpherson tartans. The sett of the Dress Macpherson was copied in 1745 by Lady Cluny-Macpherson (Hon. Jean Fraser of Lovat) from an old plaid then at the house of Cluny. The same sett, with grey ground, is the Hunting Macpherson tartan. In 1952 the Macphersons opened the first ever exclusively clan museum at Newtonmore; it is situated at the junction of the Loch Laggan and Inverness roads.

Old Hunting Macrae

Though the Gaelic *Mac Rath* ('son of grace') has pious connotations the clan became known as 'MacKenzie's Shirt of Mail' in their capacity as bodyguard to the MacKenzies of Kintail, Ross-shire. As Chamberlains of Kintail, Vicars of Kintail, and Constables of Eilean Donan Castle (from 1520 onwards) the Macraes zealously protected the MacKenzies and Kintail. In 1539 Donald Mac-Donald of Sleat brought 50 galleys to attack Eilean Donan and an arrow from Duncan Macrae, one of the three men holding the castle, fatally wounded the MacDonald chief. A Macrae compiled the 17th-century Gaelic Fernaig Manuscript.

MOTTO: *Fortitudine (With fortitude)*.

Macrae of Conchra (Sheriffmuir)

The Rev. John Macrae of Dingwall (1614–73), a son of Farquhar, vicar of Kintail, founded the Macraes of Conchra, a family known for its long association with the British army. This tartan is based on the sett of a kilt thought to have been worn at Sheriffmuir in 1715. Sheriffmuir was an indecisive conflict between Jacobite Earl of Mar and Hanoverian Duke of Argyll at which almost all the Macraes present were killed. There was no clan participation in the '45. In 1932 a Macrae of Conchra, Lieut.-Colonel John Macrae-Gilstrap, completed the restoration of Eilean Donan Castle after acquiring the ruins.

MOTTO: *Fortitudine (With fortitude)*.

Menzies

This name, in its earliest form, was distinguished when, in 1249, Alexander III appointed Sir Robert de Meyners Lord High Chamberlain. His son, Alexander, obtained Weem and Aberfeldy and, as a reward for supporting Bruce, the baronies of Glendochart and Durisdeer. In 1715 and 1745 the Menzies clansmen, if not their chiefs, were solidly Jacobite. The 16th-century Castle Menzies at Weem, Perthshire, was the clan seat until 1910 when the direct family line ended: .in 1957 the Menzies Clan Society bought the castle to restore it. Menzies of Culdares introduced the larch to Scotland in 1738.

MOTTO: *Vill God I zall (Will God I shall)*.

Murray of Atholl

The 1st (Murray) Earl of Atholl was created 1629 and the 2nd Earl, John, became Marquis of Atholl and a confirmed Jacobite. The 2nd Marquis, John, became Duke of Atholl and a confirmed opponent of the parliamentary Union of 1707. Lord George Murray, the son of the Duke of Atholl, masterminded all the military victories in the '45 but, because he advised retreat from Derby, came to be blamed by Bonnie Prince Charlie for all the failures of the Rising. Lord George was threatened when he tried to see the Prince in exile. Blair Castle, Perthshire, home of the Duke of Atholl, dates from 1269 and is now open to the public in the summer.

MOTTO: *Tout prêt (Quite ready)*.

Robertson

The Clan Donnachaidh originally took its name from Donnachaidh Reamhar (Fat Duncan), a stout friend and supporter of Bruce at Bannockburn. The present name derives from Duncan's grandson, Robert, who apprehended Sir Robert Graham for the murder of James I and had his lands erected into the Barony of Struan in 1451 as a reward. The career of Alexander, 17th of Struan, 'the Poet Chief', illustrates the clan's legendary enthusiasm for the Stuarts. He fought under Dundee in 1688, supported the Old Pretender in 1715, and at 85 put the clan at the disposal of Bonnie Prince Charlie in 1745.

MOTTO: *Virtutis gloria merces (Glory is the reward of valour)*.

Scott

The first recorded Scottish Scott was 12th-century Uchtredus filius Scoti, ancestor of the Scotts of Buccleuch and the Scotts of Balwearie. By the end of the 15th century the Scotts were powerfully established and well able to look after themselves in the Border Raids. The great novelist Sir Walter Scott, a descendant of the Scotts of Raeburn, made a unique contribution to the history of tartans when he personally organised, in 1822, the first visit to Scotland by a reigning monarch since Charles II. George IV wore Highland dress and expected the chiefs to do likewise. It was the interest created by this visit that initiated the tartan industry.

MOTTO: *Amo (I love)*.

Royal Stewart

Although associated with crown rather than clan this tartan is much worn for there is no crown copyright on its use. The Stewarts descended from 12th-century Walter, High Steward of Scotland, whose family became hereditary High Stewards. Through marriage to Marjory—Robert the Bruce's daughter—Walter, 6th High Steward, produced the first Stewart king, Robert II. On the death of Bonnie Prince Charlie's brother, Cardinal York, the male line ended. Historically the official tartan of the Royal House of Scotland, it was described by George V as 'my personal tartan'.

MOTTO: *Virescit vulnere virtus (Courage grows strong at a wound)*.

Hunting Stewart

Despite its name, this is not a clan Stewart tartan and can thus legitimately be worn by those with no clan or sept or district claim to a tartan. Hunting setts, like the green Hunting Stewart, were worn to afford some camouflage for hunters in the heather. They were evolved by those with conspicuously bright clan tartans. The Hunting Stewart is now regarded as a national hunting tartan and, though worn by the Royal Scots, has no military associations. Unlike the Royal Stewart, this tartan has no personal connection with the Royal Family; because of this and its lack of clan significance it is logically available to any British subject who wants to adopt a tartan.

Wallace

Though possibly derived from a Latin epithet for 'Welsh' there is now no more powerfully emotive Scottish name than Wallace. Well might Burns appeal to 'Scots, wha hae wi' Wallace bled'. In the 12th century the family established itself in Ayrshire and Renfrewshire and Sir William Wallace (1272–1305) was born near Paisley. Wallace, the Lion of Scotland, defeated the English at Stirling in 1297 and became Governor of Scotland, though it was not long before his enemies conspired to betray him into the hands of Edward I. His execution at Smithfield provided the movement for Scottish independence with its greatest martyr.

MOTTO: *Pro libertate (For liberty)*.

Douglas

It is for their extraordinary individualism that the Douglases are celebrated. Sir James, 'Black Douglas', Bruce's closest friend at Bannockburn, died in Spain with his king's heart in his possession. James, 2nd Earl of Douglas, who fell at Otterburn in 1388, is the original of Scott's *Marmion*. After accepting a dinner invitation to Edinburgh Castle in 1440 William, 6th Earl, was beheaded by his hosts. James II murdered William, 8th Earl, at Stirling Castle in 1452 and in reprisal the 9th Earl sacked Stirling. The persistent Douglas challenge to the king ended in defeat at Arkinholm in 1455 when the earldom was forfeited. Modern chemical dyes give the strong colours of ordinary Douglas tartan (*above left*). The Ancient tartan (*above centre*) uses vegetable dyes to simulate the pastel shades of the earliest tartan, whose colours would have to have been derived from local plant roots. In the Reproduction tartan (*above right*) mellow, muted colours give an impression of antiquity and exposure to the elements.

MOTTO: *Jamais arrière (Never behind)*.

R.C.A.F.

After the Second World War the Royal Canadian Air Force decided to create its own pipe band and applied to the Lord Lyon King of Arms for an appropriate tartan. It had already used the Anderson so the Lord Lyon approved a design retaining this sett and line formation but changing the dyes.

Russell

Some people prefer to stress their family background rather than their clan connection. The Russell tartan, which probably originated with the Galbraiths, has for many years been used by four different families all of whom are associated with the north-east of Scotland: the Russell, Galbraith, Hunter and Mitchell families.

Thomson

In 1958 Roy Thomson, the newspaper owner, whose grandfather, a builder-mason, had emigrated to Canada from Peebles, asked the Lord Lyon to record a tartan for 'The Thomson of that Ilk', a tartanless Border family. The Thomson tartan is based on that of another Campbell of Argyll sept, the MacTavish.